ve the water

an idyll green companion

when love ends be the water

(e.p.)

when love ends
be the water

rene villanueva

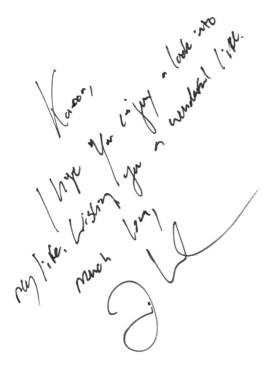

capitalist pug publishing
san antonio

I want to thank everyone who encouraged this book. a collection of my life and everyone in it until now. all the good. all the terrible. all the places and people who helped make those strange dreams with me.

a big thanks goes to my mom, dad and brothers (who lifted me as a writer and shaped this idea with their brilliant music), my wife and kids, my friends who have have been there with me (too many to count), and the amazing writers and readers i have had the pleasure to meet on social media.

the biggest thank you to rikkianne for her illustrations and vision to bring these words to a new form. I couldn't be more grateful.

to rachel and the kids
the only dream worth having

contents

one / when love ends

    queen of the barroom 3
    4 days in sa 5
    younger dreams - down the street 6
    jukebox gentleman 7
    skin naked tele - visions 19
    satori: from a bar fight an' a new black eye 21
    becoming 22
    movement one 24
    movement two 26
    movement three 27

two / some present, some now

moonlit. magic 31
side glance 35
we're all seeded 36
of form 38
lyra 39
deviant phrases 40
kiss me, bloody 42
these slow delicate sways 43
some quick thoughts go off with the storm 45
some present, some now 47
this dream 48
the many deaths left 49

three / be the water

when first I saw you 53
summer fruit 54
our - self 55
b e th e fe e l in g 56
be the water 57
when again you read 62

four /

about rene 65
about rikkianne 67

once I saw her hand
moving slow - a brush of spring
now I spill lifetimes
on this wide - flung field
waiting for her delicate turn back

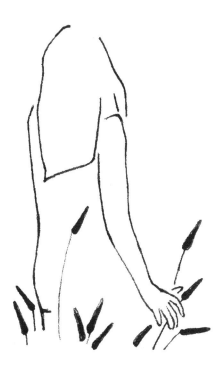

one / same thing happens

queen of the barroom

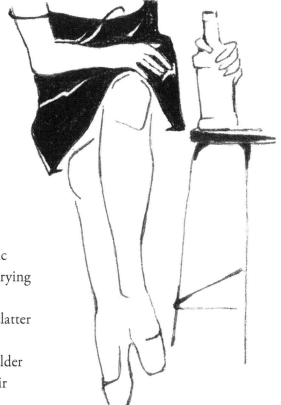

it's hard to talk music
but that's what I'm trying

high over hum and clatter
lit like moonlight
rolling her bare shoulder
open against the chair

whatever thought I had
fell off
in the darkness
under --

she is music...

some song,
I knew like love or more
I've sung too many songs
about her to remember one

it's hard to talk music
but that's what I'm trying

imagining while she stirs
her glass with rattles of ice

falling quick lashes
write runs
lines smooth
from shoulder
sweeping the soft
bend of her elbow
down to her fingers. my
heart jumping the
                    break

it'd been four days since I sent you a text
four days of no response waiting
four days of friends saying
- *rene you look miserable,* and - *what next?*
  what next? how do I what next in four days? with four days of
- *you need to get out more,* and - *you're nice enough when you try*
shit a friend says

it only took one night south
trying before it all went bloody-south
how a pacifist like me gets punched
trying to fight my way
now don't blame his fist with a high-school ring
a glory- daze ghost fed on regretting
and don't blame Sarah trapped to a ghost
who looked for life and found in me

a moment   she deserves more than a death-love
most and only I blame me still hung up on beer and four days
living to forget the ways I'd rather be in bed with you
than trying

of your candied hair
twirling thoughts of thursday silent
with smoke and laughter — unaware
of any dreams you made

I saw us, once again
we were younger

a dream down the street
by a fire burning
autumn ash
by a bed of ocher
turquoise and beryl

penetrating the ground
with sharpened fingers
in every fit and twist

melting breaths and
beads of chained
thoughtless words
and fucks dissolving
into thursday sweat

as whatever fear-fire burns
against my back

jukebox gentleman

I should've known how it was going to end before Chuck and his friends spit and cursed - *this faggot* or *mexican faggot* or whatever phrase they loved to hurl. I should've known before there was nowhere to run, there is never a where I should run.

If I could've read the unsaid history of words hanging in the room, I would've known before. If, like me, you don't believe in fate, you might believe in this chemical inevitability. A life where things set long before are just waiting for the right combination to react. And so we came to be in the piss yellow glow of the jukebox witnessing. All parts moving to an end.

Chuck sniffed - keep the fuck away from Sarah. And I said - I didn't. Sarah rolled her eyes and said over me – fuck off Chuck. We were all the wrong combinations pushing together. With the all the fire of a football chant Chuck repeated over and over - *do you know where you are?* I asked - *if I was queer than what would it matter if I was around her?* I felt the heat of anger burn in the air and yeah, I know it was a dumb thing to say… words fail, when people fail words.

- This ain't about you, or not completely.

After the me I knew left with you, I needed something to happen. The whole week had been falling towards this. Cause of who they are. And where we live. And the number of drinks. And the song that was playing. And all the years past. Or the dinner he had. And the shit that's on TV right now. This President, or the last one, or the next.

All the labels that divide our country. Or the last four days moping wanting something different than - *no answer*. And all the words that hang on my body. And cause I'm the kind of dude who waits and dreams of lying all day in bed with a love that is happy with enough. But enough doesn't come by waiting. And that big fist'll come swinging around, Invisible Hand of America, to name me. Even as I felt it all coming. I waited. Wondering when this fist became inevitably linked to my jaw.

◊

What am I alone? Some newly unemployed, college burn out. Alone again except a moleskine stuffed with half-ideas, and always worried why I hadn't done anything great yet. No, I couldn't be home staring at a blank screen for your text I knew wasn't coming. I needed change in any direction. And I needed it faster than life was leading. So it came to be I skipped my usual attempt to not hunt for work and spent my last twenty on beer instead of a meal.

Tuesday. Six-thirty-something at a little fox hole bar. A beat cinder shack in the woods stuck in the perpetual strangeness of midnight. Black barred windows. Jukebox hum waiting for the next coin drop as cold blue and white miller neon split dim over a well-worn pool table. And Sarah was there. All rhythm and mood. Here, in my words, she is only a half-remembered song. Honestly we barely knew each other. I don't even know if she knew my name. She only called me Gentleman, cause she knew I liked to read and always let her order first.

We'd a matching love for Booker T., Lee Hazlewood, Johnny Nash and Sir Doug but honestly she'd dance with anybody if they're nice enough to buy a round. And if no one would, she'd dance by herself, usually to the calls of men like the bartender and the old trailer park cowboys, and the lawyers and doctors who run here late avoiding their homes.

My brothers had told me to get out more - maybe then ya won't write so many sad songs. My heart told me to hide away. Yelp said it had the cheapest specials I could walk to. But it's all really just another ingredient to the mixture.

- Ya can't taste a difference right? The bartender looked me over with an odd disgust after I ordered my second Lone Star Light. - Why d'ya order Light?

I shrugged.

- It's the same fucking beer.

The old man stared at me waiting for some unknown response then gave up with a sigh when I shrugged again.

At some point I learned it's not about beer choices. Or looks. Or who you love. Or what you do. Or your last name, skin tone or genealogy. There are people lining the walls and filling the tables of every bar around the country. Guys still wearing high school glory-day rings and yelling to turn off the music so they can stare at whatever game is most important this week. Women who want to be seen and held the way they were before debt and fiscal safety eroded away their passion to be. Guys slowly dying in suburbia with nothing to do about

- Be nice to my gentleman.

The old buzzard only shook his head

- What ya' want babe?

Sarah ordered her whiskey neat with this blank stare. That kind of nothing-yet-everything- model-beauty she wore easily as she ran her fingers through the back of my hair like a mindless habit. And when I finally came back and caught her look that pierced something deep and made me remember the text I sent and how I was alone and did not want to be alone. It made me want to write a song and left my whole spine tingling with unexpressed possibilities of being. If only I'd had a few good words for this feeling it would have been a song.

- Not much for talking? She smiled like my quietness didn't mother her and that felt like kindness.

The old man finally put together a glass of ice and whiskey, then begrudgingly opened a blue can, holding it tight with a dead stare to me, then to the pool table before finally releasing.

Sarah nodded for help getting out of her fringe jacket. Moving slow, the jacket rolled off her bare shoulder. Revealing only a single freckle on her milk white shoulder. Her blonde hair rolling down in waves. Somehow I focused back enough to pay, and she noticed my notepad out my back pocket while I fumbled with my wallet.

- I heard you write.

- Only when inspiration comes. I said sounding cooler and more self-important than I intended, - and so far not tonight.

- Well... let's find you some then.

Balancing drinks in hand we curved to the soft light of the jukebox. Past the pool tables where Chuck and his two friends were shooting. Sarah knew her numbers by heart and by the time the first CD qued we were rocking side to side.

- Look how nicely the gentleman dances. She said working her way closer to me.

- You mean this? I laughed attempting a turn and spilling some beer between us.

- Really? Chuck yelled to his friends or the whole bar - that Fuck?!

Rolling back the left sleeve of his beige work shirt and eyeing me for one of those long seconds before he went back to his game with another crack. The cue ball slammed around the table as his shot sunk into a side pocket. Setting his next shot he added lowly - Wouldn't even know what to do with her.

– Don't worry. Sarah brushed it off, with a roll of her eye. - I don't... she trailed off as if to say what's gotten into him tonight without saying it.

– Doesn't bother me.

I kept dancing. It didn't bother me. I could still drink and dance. And for me it was all but forgotten by the next laugh. No I don't think it bothered me. Two songs and three-quarters of a drink went by with Sarah when she pulled me across the bar and asked me to hold her glass and jacket as she went to the bathroom, and again my name,

- Be a gentleman, would you?

I looked around the bar. For what? I don't know. Maybe you? Maybe my brothers who said they'd just left the apartment? Chuck's friends still watching from the pool table making a joke.

So I went with her and waited. Holding our drinks and her coat. Listening to music and the sporadic crack of pool balls. A couple laughing. A young girl at the bar talking to the TV about a baseball game. Chuck and the bartender. I mulled over words thinking of a way to start a poem like Sarah. Queen of the Bar. But it felt impossible. There were maybe 5 guys here who would probably like to push me aside to be with her right now. Guys who would know some clever thing to say. And me with my desire for words, and all the books and poems I've read, and songs of love, have nothing.

Like my head's empty.

I didn't know it yet, but I couldn't start because it's never enough to want something. Like a poem. Like Sarah. I hadn't gone through enough, to her or him or them or whatever I want. Bad starts. Embarrassments. Dead ends. Wrong turns.

Mistakes I hadn't made. I didn't know. So I waited. An empty vessel. For something else to pour into. Some perfect words that'll never come. Waiting for everything. Waiting. I was stuck in my dead stare when then, like she knew what I didn't, Sarah came back changed. A new rhythm. A new song. Life. Maybe it was her hair, or maybe she was wearing new lipstick? Or maybe I was just seeing her for the first time? A change in her. In me? What did I know about looks?

- Have you ever seen somebody you want, want you back? It's devastating.

I remember I fought to keep my heel from jittering as Sarah walked to me and my back hit the wall as she came in close to grab her drink and jacket. As her eyes fed back and forth between mine, her bare shoulder pouring out of the shadow, she must have seen it in me too cause she smiled like I hadn't seen her smile before. Suddenly the last four days of loneliness burnt away completely as she inched closer to me. Shortening my breath with her distance. Feeling her leg slid against mine. Our hands reaching to each other as she gave me a kiss. Then another as she broke her grip. Her eyes wildly red. Her breath hot with hunger, spit and whiskey. My hand fell to the small of her back, as hers slid across my face and everything went electric. - for being... you.

Her lips returned to mine. And there was only movement and feeling. The pulse and rush of blood together. Breath in between beats. Fingers delicate reached to my chest. Pushing her thigh to my leg. Trying to get close. Every part of me reaching to her. And in a moment where my mind was scattered across sensation. I felt her linger a breath against my my lip before she pulled away.

- Don't make a thing about it. She warned as her hand slid one last time up and down my thigh. As she left, her lips took me with her. A part of me still clung to that endless smile as she danced herself back to the bar.

Dumbfounded. I stood at the back of the bar. Lost in time. For how long? The sounds of the night echoed away. Like the strangeness of midnight in the dark with my head swirling. Thinking about the taste of lipstick and whiskey. Thinking about Sarah and I - what would a gentleman do next?

That was when I felt his hand on my neck.

◊

Maybe I knew how it was going to end before I was thrown face first into the alley. Maybe I knew before there was nowhere to run. Maybe long before the spitting and cursing, I had turned away from the words hanging over me and the bar all night. Before he told to keep away from Sarah and she told him to leave us alone. Everyone and everything was already dead set on the outcome.

And I had nothing to do but wait. Wait for that big fist to come swinging around.

Wait.

One hit and it was over.

Turns out I didn't have a choice about getting up either. My body had decided I wasn't moving when the dirt filled my mouth. Not even when Sarah came out to the alley with a blur of words. Pacing back and forth calling Chuck a piece of shit. Whispering what I thought was an apology before she left alone.

- Gentleman.

I didn't move when Chuck laughed, picked my notebook off the alley floor. His hands thumbed through days of ideas before tearing the whole thing in two, and setting a lighter to half. Or when the bartender came out with a laugh, and a pat on the winners back as they all went inside with the heavy close of metal door.

After everything, my still busted idiot mind could only think of Sarah. Her taste like whiskey and lipstick. Her rhythm by the jukebox. Her smile in the blue and white neon.

I spit out the first chunk of blood and dirt back on the ground as notes of a familiar song came on the distant jukebox. Scrapping guitar. The happy pump of the organ and grooving bass. Things returned. My heartbeat slowed to the sudden rush of feeling.

- But what do I know about this or any feeling? Like everything was new. My phone buzzed between my jeans and the street. And again I thought it was you, only to be a text from my brothers

- almost there.

Almost worse. Almost better. My heart still beating. My body still electric. And everything hurt. I followed my newness down the alley to the edge of the street. I couldn't tell you how long I stood watching stars over the treeline as my head throbbed to the faint bass seeping through the concrete. Sometime after, Sarah came rushing past searching violently through her bag. She didn't even see me as she sped away. The air was heavy and still, hanging around choking me on the stillness. Relief came pulling up slowly.

I spat one more time on the sidewalk before I slid into the back of my brother's 57.

- Shit Mano. They both laughed as I groaned my way in. Settling into the corner of the seat. My head resting against the cool window while I flipped through your old messages again.

- Sooo... what you think Rene?

- Do I look like I want to party?

- Well you shouldn't sleep right? Besides you don't know who will be there.

We rode on to the lake with only the drone of tire and engine. The occasional highway light swept across my face. And all the good things I had started to fall away till there was only the throbbing pain in my head as I held my jaw and some memory of you and me at your house. A kiss remembered. As you touched my face. When I saw you, see me. So different. Almost.

16

that stillness her kiss brought
that good metallic pain as
blood released slowly from my lip

awake
in red night

skin naked
tele - visions
blaring wide - bands
of burning orange and yellow

exhausted
we wrapped leg
around leg. feeling
closer
      'move you...r elbo'
she huffed
  a last
lost vacuum - ous living
sound over sounds
over breathing

in
slender fingers
sliding cotton

reached
soft - dreams
below

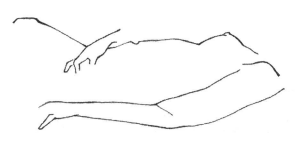

now flesh
now some autumn
holding
some - where
before couch - death news

       'could you?'

softly trailed

her lips broke red
I shook
cold
in saturday air

how many times?
I wondered that coming
death of dreams
like winter

soon

satori
(*from a bar fight
an' a new black eye*)

my time I'd turn
a fist has past. have we
not cooled this yet?

are we still wet dreaming
of cowboys and bar-fights
and pistol smoke?
of hands that take by the waist
throwing tar, and blood and heat
and only wanting to take?

didn't we learn
hands only temper at the end
of a western and any hands
that take with hate
can only give with hate?

and when he laid it on me
scraped knuckle
to blistering eye
I only returned

a laugh -
my time I'd turn
a fist has past

1

the parts of me unknown,
equal to myself, you
divided and understood

with all the pieces held now
a better whole

2

under the same moon
where flies a night bird and I
lazing dreams like summer

near, by the bend in your
legs and skin soaking

how good it is to be here
sharing under the same moon?

3

she's a heaven to herself
no virgin. no madonna. no whore.

a golden skin heaven
a lavender heaven with purple polish

the dream of a hundred nights
                              in flesh
the dream of molecular chance
                              in jeans

4

this was not who I was when I left you
no, my own street wouldn't know my wide foreign walk
I was made new

once a body known
but that body's gone
I spilled him bloody on a page

to know
who I was

becoming

grand piano c^9
struck satin
to her beechwood bergamot
clashed a wave salt sweet
a grand piano

never saw your elegance
till then, the 9th,
elevated and discrete
  but I hear you now

before then: we rose, entangled
riding higher from lobby
fumbling for a card: the 9th
room laid out in - *c*
curving from counter kitchen
to couch, to our then comfort

follow
our   notes
laid chordal

rushed to the chorus
from a chord

from you then
a grand piano
struck satin c^9

among woodwinds
outside a sea swell rush
lifted the drift of people. laughter
golden in sun golden in mind
a thousand jeweled laughter
laid on beach towels
and naked knees
elbows painted in sand
reflections of unaware american - isms
reached from there to here

our stage, a balcony,
an open window
a curtain covering two in tune
then falling back on our lotus - bed -
flower as we dove deeper aglow
          in beautiful, warm, melody - less sleep

a knock. my heart
a dream or the next part?

1, 2, 3...
called off his knuckles
turned soft looks like doped eyes, to panic
cause no. our end won't come by a hum or a rattle
but a knock

and you'd know his sound anywhere
and you knew it deep in the daze of our song

running now. elegant phrases
pieced together follow
the notes

here a sock, here a purse, a bra,
his heat from the door

a movement. off the heavenly balcony
9 floors over blissful sand
when a vast ocean breathes
a cooling wind
against a knock

but our song didn't end a crescendo of tears or blood
-- it's much quieter than that

settled vibrations in a lost hall
dissipate down the damping carpet
her hair turned
her hips and at last a heel
to the elevator
down the 9th

she's gone
a wave salt sweet
a grand piano
struck satin c^9

two / some present, some now

you said, when you first saw me smile, really smile, a depth appeared you'd never seen on me before, and that's when you knew. but women never reveal themselves so easy. I think that's why I can't remember... there was no one moment. you grew on me, so gradually, I didn't notice when there was nothing else but you.

Driving up, my jaw ache finally started to subside. Under stars and headlights flashing. Surrounded by laughter from some people I knew, or didn't. The muddy thump of music from a distant car stereo as my brother's parked the car. I gave a couple of hellos and found a cold drink I could rest against my face. Moonlit. Everything relaxing. Old dreams move slow. If I closed my eyes I knew - You were somewhere. *This party. Again. Like when we met.*

◊

Somehow we'd drifted together, among the lost bodies. Talking longer than I usually do with anyone. Somehow after a few hours of floating between conversations, we sat shoulder to shoulder in the cooling night when against my will I was put in charge of rolling a joint, and you laughed brilliantly and I thought your voice had a beautiful sound, even when it was mocking me. And that's still true. You make songs in loving, hating, fighting or fucking. You make all sounds beautiful in themselves.

- That's really fucking hideous Rene. Start again.

- It's utilitarian, I said. Already flooded with a wonderful embarrassment as I tried to light the end of the paper and only producing more laughter.

- Is that what you are? A utilitarian?

- Function isn't a bad quality you know?

- Function? No... mood over. Try again. You made this look of disgust but in the second after, I swear I saw you bite your lip. Or am I just remember it happening?

- How are you an adult, Rene and can't roll? Fuck! No wonder you're alone.

It was Bullard. He emerged from the party, circled the fire, took the ugly disaster I created and tore it apart. Squatting over his boots and pressed wranglers with his finger nails black with grease he set to rebuilding.

- I thought this shit was like... your people's thing.

- What the hell y'talking about Bullard?

- I know you're like, one of the good ones, but you know? *Mary-juan-a* rene. He lit up underneath his trucker hat, with that country smile and the glow of his blonde-red beard in the fire that seemed to disappear at times and re-emerge to make his round boyish face have a little dirt to it.

- *What?* You said, holding back any hint of civility. And I couldn't help but laugh.

- Don't. I shook my head wanting that question die among the flames as he finished and passed the joint to you.

- Alright. Alright. Bullard lifted his hat and handed his newlcrafted piece back to me with a half smile. - You're welcome.

With a nod, he disappeared from my memory into the mass of people moving in and out of car lights. Walking shadows off to the woods.

- Don't get him going about race or that won't end till tomorrow. I said. And I wondered what that stare you gave meant as the smoke fell out of your mouth.

Your eyes came back from somewhere else and you asked - Don't you want to get out of this?

- Don't we all?

- Yeah but they can't. You... I heard about you.

You took another drag and closed your eyes. The silence filled with the sounds of the burning pile. Pieces of dried branches breaking apart into the whole. The light flickering across your face. And behind you the low moon seemed to halo around your hair.

- I'm stuck like anybody else here. The words fell out of my mouth into the fire.

The flames burned down. And we moved on to other things. Your roommate's need to walk around in only a towel. My band's possiblity of a possiblity. Using a stick to prod embers as the fire finally started to fade, and drawing your name in the dirt before you got up, leaving me on the decrepit log which felt like forever then but I can't remember now. Some moments lost in the night magic. Then you came back and opened your purse and pulled out a third of Johnny Walker you stole from your parents house.

33

- Not here. You whispered and threw a look of trouble over to the woods. And I followed you hand in hand to the river edge.

a few moments after and your bare-
knee bumped against my leg

clothes thrown on a dare

a smoke, a swig and a laugh
nothing to hold but each other

moonlight pouring
on the river

around us

- a kiss

the side-glance
an important tool
    for learning love

a quick look
not long
  where unseen

                you see

is she's staring back?
does she moves her lips when she reads?
does she twirls the curls of her brunette dreams?

never too long

even when she's back
in your room with her back to you
- and though she knows - with a smile

you might glimpse
how she shakes a skirt
or her pout as she re-strikes
her lipstick before
coming
back

bodies hungry for sun. waiting. out of season
for every kink, break
and deviation

waiting to grow
waiting for change
waiting to cut layers that bury our beauty
waiting
in beds
in winter
exhausted

I burst east and sun-hunting came low
to find your hand
waiting. now

--close your eyes?
--did you feel me?
--did you feel a breeze pushing
the window bringing us
the scent of rosemary?
-- I didn't know it was, yet it bloomed

yet
our fingers
easily slide against each other
        fit almost like they've
been waiting

we're all seeded
only knowing
we will grow
but not how
not how long

ours
side by side
out of season
hungry for sun

for now I'd like to stay

side
by
side

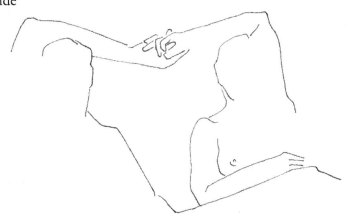

run the curve of her spine
move gently with her
down the back of her leg
knowing she's all truth

I read it to read her
a real poet of form

with her I'd go beyond every lined-horizon
follow changes
dance in phrase to her

my desire to live her space
a feeling that kills
fills me

cause I am for her,
every word hung in a moment

I can know myself
at the edge of her finger
I can travel over her shoulder
and off

to that eternal
       understanding

lyra/look
our gold evening
like friends and drunk summer laughter

follow
the walk
the water
the smooth stones
a circle made
don't I love to see her
stretch the sky and smile -
when she sings music we're too afraid to play

I
laugh to wish to be so free as her
and say, myself more, naked
like babies in the frio
she makes strangers love themselves stronger
- that is her magic -

lyra/look
our gold evening
like drunk summer laughter

deviant phrases burn thru minds
on the wide field-track
behind the high school
where we huddled
around that single-smoke rising
laughing ideas of futures unknown

I held it in, cause the first to cough
might be dead five years down
I held it in, cause we all disappear
I held it in, cause we have visions
more precious than lapsing youth

walking home through the mud
like no - thing but a passing impression
on the earth. and what will I leave
worth more than these tracks?
and who will give more than ground?

questions that burn like ether

lifted and gone

I know my fears
I've learned to whisper questions
to the sky and never out loud
to a women like Sarah, draped on
jukeboxes Sarah, illustrated
and read Sarah, sad song
of her city

she is more than an answer
she's lost more of Love than anyone here
Sarah, I know now my fears

the mud track moved me
down an underpass
an unknowing rumble growing
shadowed by multitude
where inna ditch, a huddled mass of life
came to bleed the earth one last

I can listen. Here. A breath.

I moved in a moment
off this passing dream of flesh
that all I am, a cell
of this wide earth dividing

kiss me bloody

I write poems an' watch friends go
                    lo -- my truth be bloody

no matter how beautiful I want this
                    good drinks turn to vomit

let's stop now an' both be filtered clean
                    or really kiss each other bloody

above me
amber eyes glint like
distant cities
rolling away
in map-less motion

moving
our wheel gripped tight
turns

the road hot
hums in midnight
down from rib

to navel

to hip

to

-- wait

resting
in her
aromatic landscapes
her slope and curve

falling light
collapsing over
taking only
breaths

feeling the ground swell - shiver
under fingers tracing

these slow
delicate
sways

to where --

like the horizon line
lies against the sky

-- lies her thigh tonight

some quick thoughts go off with the storm

the old cock, with
her weather
came
turn the vein south
with all bullish thunder
burning
her breath
she lay to me, where
slid the floor

this small fire-
feeling turning
her chest over
spreading book
down on bare breast
above

-- don't understand where
you find your dirty mind
--don't understand where
your cock goes headstrong along
sliding words to the edge
ready to fall
off
    the
        page

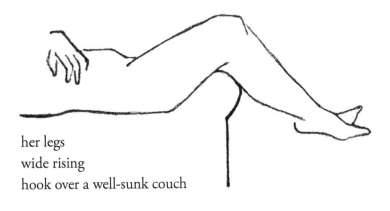

her legs
wide rising
hook over a well-sunk couch

-- and where was this?

she leaned to me an' laughed

-- have you ever heard her leaves laugh in the rising wind?

as rain filled in quickly
against her fingers
trickling those few
fortunate falls
sounds gently
wood and wind
an'a new season's storm
reading and turning

this is all
for me to be
whatever form that pours

falling to this glass or that

to try and taste then
some present, some now
made together

mixing moment
by

moment

tasting drop
by

drop

we can
make then
something good
out of this

whiskey-night and a kiss

this dream
we walked
again and I
came back

walking in hand, in halls
of you or

to you...

I could laugh
at this late-hour
knowing soon again, this dream

the many deaths left

damn bottle splintered across our would - be kitchen
long, she'd been gone when I'd found three drops of blood
from her heel

one, by a coffee spill to the handle head
one, by the turn in our hall
one, before the door - well leaving

every time I lived and died again
cleaning the last goodbye she'd said a time before
words trapped an' remembered
in the air of bleach

I hadn't cried till I thought of the many deaths left

three / be the water

when first I saw you

humming a tune
once I'd forgotten
ripe notes poured
across your lips
shaking loose, a
song-sweet floating memory
formed from inside
the desire for a body lost

making life by some
ethereal cloud
no I can't tell
what she dreamed or where
her wide-side-smile went

gone in the flick of her wrist
memory slipped
from the space gasped

between her and a song

it was her flesh
cool and lifting
eyes naked
open in slice
where we hid nothing
from our thoughts
in hunger

wet hands
dripping to elbow
in summer heat
diffusing in day
a smile burst open
ripe for eating

- I've always had
a taste for citrus
I thought drinking
through the sting

cut down my left middle
finger moved deeper in
the flesh that fruit enjoyed
together now. in summer.

our - self
your fingers slide against
my hand, mirrored
your cell - soft glide, lying life against
itself   eroding the little difference between
    the river and the granite, the bond,
  the break, we love in the friction felt between
our - self

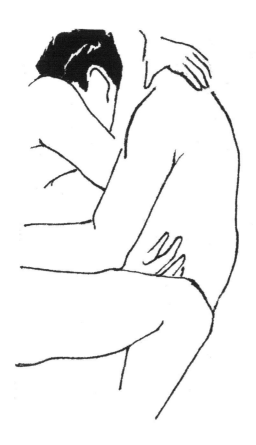

b e th e fe e l in g

cr as h bl u e
 mi n d a flood
  of su g ar an' sy na ps e
m elte d d o w n   t he
   e ve n in g s h e
d ra n k. li ke t he h ollo w
       str aw I   a m

I pou r
I e m p ty
I disp e   rs e

The feeling in my jaw came back pulsing.

*This was not the time before. If you were here I hadn't
found you, and this party seemed duller. Half the people I didn't
know. And the others, I didn't want to see. The night had lost
direction or maybe that's just me now?*

A few had come asking about a fight and the blood on
my shirt.

- Getting punched once... An' falling down ain't a fight.
That was the usual take away, or something like, - Why didn't
you hit'em back? I would've fought back.

Everybody agreed they would've fought back. It was
the right thing to do - at least throw a punch man.

These are the dreams of our city. Small places have a
thirst for blood. They chant it from the football stands, write
it in headlines, in news-feeds and tattoo it on bodies. They
build monuments to it. Carry dead flags for old wounds no
matter what truth it carries, what horrors, or hells. It's a sad
southern song. *Fight, win or die, but Fight.*

*everybody wants to drive for something. everyone wants. and
when there is nothing to challenge the mind, there's flesh. always
flesh. everyone imagines themselves the best. the strongest.
the smartest. everyone thinks they'd stand last. oh, the lies
we're told. everyone has a chance to be a winner. but there
are always more losers than winners. cause they come easy.*

There was worse advice.

- Next time strike first. Right in the throat. They won't be able to breath. Or they'd dance around some kind of drunken technique for fighting. By the fourth and fifth time I was tired of my own story. I don't know what I was expecting. Small places with a big thirst.

I grabbed a beer from a random ice chest and held it to my face. Feeling the night air as I made my way to lean against a tree. Closing my eyes and feeling like the whole world was swaying.

- A little early to be this bad Rene. What happened to you? Brianna leaned against the tree with me as we both watched the party from a distance. One hand in a big, worn herringbone coat the other carefully trying to carelessly hang a cigarette to the side.

- I got punched Bri… why are you hiding?

- You know how I like a party. She laughed. Maybe in the dark she thought I was joking or maybe she didn't want to answer the question either - You're just gonna mope forever about her then?

- It hasn't, even been a week. The words fell away unconvincingly, before I finally opened my beer. And stared at the distant fire. And other people having talks. Drinking. Getting closer.

- Well... she's moved on. Got a place in Austin, Brianna's words hung in the dark for a second. I didn't even know how to feel about that. - So maybe you should too.

- Go to Austin? What do you know about moving on Bri? You've been with one person since high school.

- Don't make it about me.

- What do want me say?

I felt the words lock up and she looked at me like you did. Again I couldn't finish it. Again I lost the words like *I need you.* Songs are written at the ends of those kinds of sentences.

- That's your problem. Right there. Bri rolled her eyes in a puff of smoke.

The bridge of my nose began to throb again. She didn't protest as I wandered away through a small path in the trees.

Walking again.

I could almost see you ahead of me. Flashing a smile in the moonlight. As we pushed on through a narrow tangle of bare sticks. Hand in hand. Until the sounds of the party were too faint to care. Only shadows around us, and we came to the edge of the river. Barefoot we touched the edge of the water and listened to the water lapping while you poured two drinks from your purse.

Nothing was said, that didn't have to be. It was in your eyes. And all I had to do was follow. You stripped down to purple bike shorts under your dress and a black sports bra. I threw down my shirt and jeans to the muddy rocks and stepped barefoot to the river. Rocks cutting against me as my body shivered in the cold. You were already swimming away.

We had the water dancing. We had the star song. We had the dream every winter branch near us had. Soon. A spring soon, with everything to come. All things wonderful reflecting over bodies like the water, your bare shoulder, and my chest.

I could almost laugh a tear
standing again, alone.
by the water

everything we'd be
was there. hiding away in winter
waiting.

- *i dare you.*

in the river

- *i dare you.*

to be nothing but our skin
soaking the cold, slow current
let the sky read our truth

- *i dare you.*

and wrote this all to you
on the water

what did you think when again,
you read?

was it the
beginnings or ends
or the times between

like I

we could be

over and again
I wonder

where d'you

love me best?

would you let me hold you there again?

four /

Rene came to his love of language hiding away in local used book stores. Choosing to devour American classics like Hemingway, Fitzgerald, and Steinbeck, over his coursework, Rene quickly moved into poetry and became fascinated by the styles of imaginst, romanitic, modernist and beat poetry. After graduating high school at 15, Rene studied English and American Literature at UTSA, taking every course he could handle (*World Religion, Folk Tales, American Short Stories, British Lit, Arthurian Lit, and a survey of poetry*). Rene began writing short stories, lyrics and poetry of his own all while interning at the local SATX publisher Gemini Ink and teaching at a community writing lab. But it was his song lyrics that took off first with the band Hacienda, where Rene spent the next few years traveling the world, singing, and writing 3 albums of songs all the while developing his skills in poetry and spoken word. Rene publishes his prose on Instagram (@hacienda_tx), keeps a journal distributed through a local Texas zine called The Word Is A Bell, and started a new musical project Idyll Green with his brothers.

Rikkianne Van Kirk is inspired by the rich past of found materials. With nothing more than some old paper (often peppered with the frustrations, musings, or desires of its previous owners) and a drugstore sharpie, her goal is to bring each page to life with simple illustrations.

Her deep appreciation for the history of these materials and her illustrative take on them has been shared and acknowledged by clients such as Paul Smith and The Kurt Vonnegut Memorial Library.

With a single black marker and some forgotten paper, Rikkianne's pieces strive to embrace the simplicity and imperfection of the hand drawn line. Ultimately breathing life into something old, something forgotten, something sentimental.

Made in the USA
Middletown, DE
17 November 2018